# Bunnies, Babies and Brides

Tales and Tidbits to Treasure
Compiled by Lisa Cristofich

Copyright © 2024 Lisa Cristofich

All rights reserved. No part of this document may be copied or distributed without permission.

ISBN: 9798320819815

# DEDICATION

Thanks to Sara Bittner who self-published her books
and recommended this path to me.

# CONTENTS

Acknowledgments

Foreword viii

| 1 | Bunnies, Babies and Brides | 1 |
| 2 | Fishing | 6 |
| 3 | Food Fascination | 12 |
| 4 | Gardens | 21 |
| 5 | HerStory, History | 24 |
| 6 | Holidays | 39 |
| 7 | Libations | 43 |
| 8 | Life Lessons | 48 |
| 9 | Pilots | 55 |
| 10 | Travel Agents | 67 |
| | Appendix | 75 |
| | Index | 82 |

# ACKNOWLEDGMENTS

Thanks to my first readers:
Susan Shertok
President of the Delaware Accordion Club
and
Wendy Jane Wiseman
Proprietor of Wendy's Beauty Salon

Thanks to Cassidy Hanley
for tech support.
The cover looks awesome!

To JETT
I'm grateful to be on your team
xoxo

# Foreword

So, you read book 1? Yeah, me too.
My entries were Sweet & Sour and Schlitterbahn.
What? You don't remember those.
Okay, I'll wait while you go back and check.
You're back, okay.
Ready for book 2!

It's fun to read about my grandpa's childhood, his horse Pran and his friend Bepo; and my Delaware grandmother and her love for the Texas bluebonnets.

This book has more of the same anecdotes and snippets of life from our family and from other people whom my aunt knows.
Thanks for ordering this second book.
Did you know that 50% of the proceeds go to my 501(c)(3) horse rescue?! Well, it's true.

We both hope that these memories inspire you to enjoy time with those you love, share the joys and camaraderie, and maybe some of you will create your own literary legacy.

Emily Cristofich
Heritage Oak Rescue
2024

# CHAPTER 1

# BUNNIES, BABIES AND BRIDES

There were bunnies in the hut at my sister's house.
One day they became dinner.
The "kids" (Linda and Joe) asked what happened to their bunnies?!
Their dad and I said they escaped.
Dad


I remember one dance where everyone was doing the bunny hop. There was a girl in the line and her wig fell off. She didn't even know!
Sam


My mom looked so young that some people thought she was the babysitter! She would say, "These are my kids!"
Denise M


I remember holding my niece Emily when she was 10 days old.
Lisa


I babysat for a family who took me with them when they went to Connecticut for vacation.
Venus


I remember traveling to Rome to see one of my favorite cousins Ksenija and her new baby Amelia.
Lisa

I remember when my cousin Linda had
her second baby, Kelly.
I spent two weeks in Virginia Beach
as mother's helper.
I remember when my other cousin was born,
Ana in New York.
I spent the summer with them.
I was so young then, and it was scary when she cried. When my Aunt Ada and Uncle John came home, they would pay me and I would run to the store around the corner for licorice.
They were actually licorice rolls,
chewy strawberry yum!
Tina


I'm really close to my sister now.
I remember when she was 4 and I was 12,
our parents were out and I was in charge.
She would not listen when I told her to go
to bed so I tied her to the doorknob
which lasted all of 10 minutes because
my conscience got the better of me.
Denise D


I remember being on dirt roads, 10 yrs old, and driving my Papa's car. My "noni" was livid! But my papa just laughed and we all waved to her and went on our merry way in his big old car with the dried basil tucked under the visor and my baby brother yelling Ah-Boo (his word for car).
Denise B

I remember playing a job at a wedding and the
bride came up to the band and said,
"If you play one more polka, I won't pay you."
Sam

I remember going to the Gaylord Hotel,
National Harbor MD, for an Indian wedding.
I heard the ceremony cost $450,000.
They originally wanted the groom to ride in on an
elephant which would have cost $20,000.
Instead, he rode in on a white horse.
And the parents washed the groom's feet.
The bride was in a canopy-covered chair
carried by four guys.
In India, this celebration would have lasted
seven days.
In the U.S., they celebrate for three days.
Natalie

My granddaughter was invited to take part in her
cousin's wedding. When asked if she wanted to be
the flower girl, she replied,
"I want to be the Flower Girl Princess."
JoAnn

I remember our cousin Inez DeSeta was famous for
her biscuits -- actually all of her baking.
She baked all my wedding cookies.
She might have even done Tina's also.
Carol

I remember for my wedding day, it was Dad's idea for me to not wear glasses, instead to get contact lens. (Lisa remembers I was in the bathroom more than the reception.) And that morning, I also stepped back and put my shoe through the veil. Fortunately, Aunt Mickey was able to fix it.
Tina

I remember when the cutest boy in school broke up with the prettiest girl, and he wanted to talk to ME!!
I also remember when I was 15 years old at my sister's wedding; my mom set me up on a date with a 19-year-old boy. We went to a Chinese restaurant where my date was very polite. He guessed the fortune cookie would say that I would get married young. He was right, it really did happen.
Venus

I was a flower girl in this wedding that had 8 bridesmaids who were all in the same style dress but each a different color.
My dress was gold and it came with a matching doll. I still have both the dress and doll.
Lisa

I remember one wedding in which the bride had the usual princess-style gown.
For the reception she changed into a more comfortable yet elegant pantsuit ensemble.
I thought that was a clever plan.
Lisa

# CHAPTER 2
# FISHING

I remember fishing with Barba Ive and knew we
would not be successful because there were too
many porpoises and they scare the fish.
Barba Ive tried to scare them away by using the oar
and hitting at the water.
Uncle John

Barney and I would go fishing and bring home
catfish. The Kelly kids up the street loved to play
with our catch.
Uncle John

I remember going on a canoe trip
and having subs for our lunch.
I was in the back of the canoe and Dad was in front.
He brought the canoe over towards the land to stop
for lunch; I commented that it didn't seem the best
spot, that it was too steep. Dad disagreed and pulled
the canoe over and got out. Unfortunately, the area
was too steep; the canoe tipped and the subs
and I fell in. My dad was on shore laughing.
Byron

I remember Anna and Felix Konatich's restaurant in
Bodega Bay CA was closed, but they opened it for
our special visit.
They asked, Annie what kind of fish she liked.
She said, "All the seafood I can see!"
Uncle John

I remember fishing in the Delaware Bay. It was the beginning of the season. We were a half mile from the shore. We couldn't believe the water was shallow and our boat hit a sand bar and got stuck. So we tilted up the motor and took off.
I remember when Tony jumped overboard in the Indian River. The tide was strong, about eight knots. I had to start the boat and go after him because the tide took him away.
I remember when Joey caught a shark. It was struggling so much. I told Joe to give it to me and I tried to reel it in. Unfortunately, the reel broke and the pole and all went overboard.
Uncle John

Joey's version. I had the drag on the reel set to tire the shark out. But dad took the rod and flipped the release on the reel and the line spooled out wildly and got all tangled and jammed.
Then the line snapped and the shark got away. We don't know for sure it was a shark,
but it was big.
Joey

I remember when we were in Beijing, we lived in a
Radisson for one year. The hotel was a part of SAS
(Scandinavian Airlines) and for staying in the hotel
we collected enough frequent flyer points that
Ksenija and Franco went to Scandinavia for a week.
I also remember going to a Benefit Ball where we
won first prize which was a 4-day sailing vacation.
Our group was Jelka, Ksenija, Emilia,
Mira, Bratso and myself.
Besides me, our group had little nautical experience
so we hired a skipper.
Feručo

We went mackerel fishing on a charter boat. Joe was
so seasick he did not even notice that he was laying
on burlap bags full of clams for bait.
This is totally opposite of his grandfather who was a
daredevil on water.
My son, my father, and I went fishing off the coast
near Dover DE.
We were about 10 miles out where the party boats
go. We had motor trouble and had to be towed by
the coast guard. Luckily the party boats were there
to call the coast guard for us.
While waiting to be towed,
we caught two fish at a time.
Uncle John

I found a wonderful little trattoria in the mountains.
Their food is delicious, the prices are low,
and the view
from up on the mountains is incredible.
I've picked up a new hobby on the weekends –
fishing. My friend showed me a pond
where you can catch trout.
You pay for your fish, and clean the fish right there.
My friend also showed me how to cook the fish,
and it makes a delicious meal. Ever since then
I've been fishing almost every weekend.
Actually I did get tired of eating them too.
I just didn't get tired of catching them.
That was the fun part, and then you're left
with a bunch of fish that you have to prepare
and eat or get rid of somehow.
Ben

Joe, Tony and I were fishing at Indian River.
The tides were coming in and the waves were very
high.  Everyone shouted let's go back, let's turn
around. Joe and Tony were praying hard.
Instead I took the boat over a "mountain" wave
of water.  If we had been in the surf, the boat would
have capsized.  That day we brought home our
biggest catch: four foot sharks!
Uncle John

Did I tell you the story of when we went fishing and your brother was praying because he thought we were going to die? It was a day I'll never forget. We went to Indian River.

It was my Dad, Tony and me. We put the boat in the water and my dad went to park the car.

A lady said do you have your plug in your boat? It looks like it is sinking! I jumped in quickly while Tony held the rope attached to the boat. I opened the hatch, and sure enough, water was pouring in. I inserted the plug but we had quite a bit of water in the boat. My dad arrived and said, "No problem. When we get going we will open the plug and the water will be sucked out." It worked wonderfully.

Then we headed out through the mouth of the Indian River where it meets the ocean. The tide was coming in as the river flowed out. The waves were huge, I thought at the time, but probably they were about ten feet high. The boat struggled up to the top of a wave and as the wave passed by
it lifted the boat into midair.

It came crashing down with a tremendous thud as the boat hit the bottom of the wave.

The sound made you think the boat would break in half. It then struggled to the top of the next wave and the sequence repeated. Tony said, "Turn back, Uncle John." But I knew we couldn't because the boat would have capsized. It was pretty scary. Then Tony prayed for God to save us. After a few more waves we were through and out to the ocean where it was calm again.

Joey

# CHAPTER 3
# FOOD FASCINATION

I remember my neighbor Joe brought us a store pie
that had three stickers on the outside packaging
which said Blueberry Pie. As soon as I cut it, to serve
John and Tony, we all realized
there were NO blueberries in THAT pie,
it was pineapple!!
Catherine


I remember the law school dance where I wore a
beautiful outfit, soft like pajamas with long sleeves
and bell bottoms.
It was dark brown with beige piping.
Well, that long sleeve dipped right into the Russian
dressing and turned it bright red, ugh!
Sylvia


I remember one day I was in a hurry and wanted
to order a quick meal from McDonald's including a
Happy Meal which I thought would be for
my 4-year old son Jorge. "Oh no," he says to me,
"Momma, I want to go to the fish market to buy
pasta vongole (pasta with clams)."
Natalia


I remember for Saint Patrick's Day,
my mother cooked mackerel for my father
for breakfast!
Peg

I remember my ex-husband's aunt would hide
Tastykakes and other treats in the freezer.
Her husband would find this hiding place and he
would secretly take the cupcakes, go to the car,
warm them up with the car heater,
and eat them in the car.
Adelaide

I remember mom would make us chicken
sandwiches on an Italian roll or white bread,
they were so good. Dad would eat juicy fruits.
We took all these goodies to the movie theatre,
especially for *Fiddler on the Roof* that was three
hours long.
Linda A

We used to have a real special breakfast at times
in the spring: scrambled eggs with wild asparagus
and prosciutto, it was delicious.
The wild asparagus would just grow anywhere in
the woods in the spring. For dinner, we had ravioli,
spaghetti, goulash and chicken.
It was all fresh food and my mom was a good
cook; she also knitted wool socks.
My mom would let me go play all the way down
to the bottom of the valley. We had one cow and
would take it there to the pasture to
graze. We had a garden and would grow corn,
lettuce, tomatoes and all sorts of things.
My mom would cook good sauerkraut.
Dad

I remember when I was a model for my niece Lesa.
She photographed scenes with me holding an egg.
I was amazed at the number of ways there were to
actually hold the egg with one hand. She was able to
showcase her talent as the lens captured the texture
of my hand in so many ways.
The final collage was fascinating.
Nancy

I remember when I was in high school and dating
an Italian guy. I helped make the raviolis and
then realized that the gemstone had fallen out of
my ring. Well, we ate our dinner very slowly
trying to find it.
Judie

I remember Sil Stortini whose father was a chef.
He worked at the Northeast Yacht Club
(an exclusive place). Sil took me and Ann for steak
dinner. It was so tender you could cut it with a fork,
no fat!!
Dad

One May we visited Val and Chuck in California.
As we drove toward their house, we could see the
strawberry fields. It was perfect timing for the peak
of the season. They were BIG fresh strawberries, just
delicious!! Valerie had a whole cookie tray FULL of
these yummy beauties.
Tony

As newlyweds, we invited Ann and Tony to dinner at our apartment.  Since my culinary skills were not fully developed, my attempt at an apple pie turned out to be apple soup!  They never let me forget it!  Tony was always proud of his homemade wine, although Ray teased him by calling it the "best homemade vinegar" he ever tasted. Ray liked Fridays at Continental Custom Floors.  Tony always brought Ann's pepper and egg sandwiches to work.
Dot

I remember when I was a girl at home in Austria, my mom would make this yummy delectable treat. She would get a nectarine, take out the pit, then with potato dough, roll it in sugar, make a ball and bake it.  Yummy!
Mitzi

I was a bouncer at this club and the chef was making Bananas Flambé.  The fluff on front of his tuxedo shirt caught fire.
I grabbed the ice water bucket that had been holding the champagne and threw it on him.
Joe B

I love Mexican food and wanted to share the fun
with my mom and sister.
Well, they hated it!!!
I felt like I had guacamole all over me.
Larry

Sometimes 300 people were in the Club that seemed
like it could hold 3,000. There were acts like the
Platters and Diana Ross.
When Ricky Nelson sang there, only 30 people
showed up. So we threw a party at Jamie Wyeth's
house. At 7 a.m. the next morning, I cooked eggs
with garlic.
I knew my wife Barbara Ann wouldn't believe my
story, so I took them home with me. I hid in the
bushes near the front door, while Ricky Nelson and
Jamie rang the doorbell.
Joe B

My first palačinka was like food from heaven!!
Mom

Every summer, people asked me why my
tomatoes grow so tall? What do I do special?
And really the tomato is growing
to reach the sun.
Dad

### 5 memories from Tina

One year I sold the most Girl Scout cookies.
I also tried to get the most badges I could.
We went camping and I learned that making Smores was the best and coolest thing EVER.
We also made dinner at the campsite, putting all the food into aluminum foil, folding it up and letting it cook.

In the first years of marriage in the apartment,
I would study recipes and make really good dinners like
Chicken Cordon Bleu and Chicken Saltimbacca.

I remember a cake I made for DECA
(a high school leadership organization),
it looked wonderful.
Well, I put in on the back of the car, got to top of street, I stopped so suddenly and slammed on the brakes. Yikes! The cake flew off its ledge!
Fortunately, I was able to put it back together.

I remember a family vacation to Virginia Beach.
At dinner, I ordered hush puppies - yum yum!
And I still love them!

For college graduation party, I wanted a Carvel ice cream cake.  The closest Carvel ice cream store was Edgewood, MD yet even with the air conditioning on,
the cake started to melt by the time I got home.

I remember when the mechanic forgot to put the
oil plug back in, after he changed the oil,
so it sprayed all over inside the engine.
We were not allowed to ride in the tow truck,
so we had to ride from Chicago to Wilmington
in our own car.
We had a jug of pretzels and a six-pack of beer.
We took a few naps and life was good!!
Eleanor

I remember when we lived in Billings MT and we
took in foster children. Each week we would try
international dishes and the kids would help
cook. One gal made fajitas
and they tasted just awful.
I knew my two-year-old would immediately say
exactly what she thought, "yuk." So I grabbed
the bowl of sugar and coated the fajita dish
THEN the little one said, "Yum, yum."
Linda M

When I was 9 years-old, the cat would jump on
my lap and want attention so I would give it a
little piece of formaggio (cheese) and some
capicola, but not the spicy part.
Sam

I remember Corky asking for a sliver of dessert,
but then said,
"Not that small a sliver.
I want to be able to see the cake."
Tina

My dad was quite clever. I remember we had a
bakery cake and when they closed the box,
the lid made a gash along one whole side.
Joe was home from San Jose
and said, "Cut this side first."
But I did not hear him
and started on the other side.
Well, Dad quickly grabbed a spatula and
smoothed that spot with icing seamlessly.
Lisa

My uncle was a baker and would give my mom
the empty flour sacks. She would cut out a
pattern to make the smocking
trim for the front of my dress.
Etta

My husband's Aunt Mary would put the bread
"to sleep." She would cut slices, put butter there,
place the bread on a blanket and cover it.
After awhile, she would put it back in the oven.
Sometimes, she would bake bread twisted in the
shape of an eight and sometimes with anchovies.
Jean

### Jean's story from book 1
I was wearing my new black velvet dress with matching black
velvet purse. I ate some of Aunt Mary's bread and did not
know it had anchovies (yuk). When no one was looking,
I put that "bite" into my purse.
The smell ruined my new purse
and I had to throw it out.

# CHAPTER 4
# GARDENS

When we bought our house the previous owners were big gardeners.
We had a vegetable garden the size of Delaware (okay, maybe not quite that big) and another herb garden not quite the size of Rhode Island and a circle of strawberries. I would spend hours on a Saturday weeding and only get half done and do the other half the next weekend. I decided that it wasn't worth the effort because produce is not very expensive when it's locally grown and in season.

I planted an entire row of head lettuce and everyone was impressed that they grew. The only problem was that they all were ready for picking at the same time and you can only give away or eat so may lettuce heads. Sad to say, but most went bad. Since that time I found out that you stagger your planting to avoid that problem.

My brother-in-law lived with us for a couple of months and planted some potatoes.
At that point we were only using the one corner of the garden and the rest of the garden was full of waist high weeds. He moved out in the middle of the July and that summer my husband plowed the garden under. To this day we are looking for those potatoes in the yard.
Mary H

I remember going to the Italian market in
Philadelphia. Those grocers did not want you to
touch their produce.
One customer did, and the grocer threw a head of
lettuce at him!
Thelma

When I was a small child--my dad was a gardener
and we would always have this little spring snow
and he called it the onion snow for the onion bulbs
he had put in the ground.
Pat

I remember when I went to this hidden beach to
pick asparagus with my father and grandfather.
It grew wild and plentiful.
We did this for years until word got out
and the whole town came and
cleaned out the entire asparagus field,
seemingly overnight.
Richard

I remember going down the Dupont Highway.
There was a large median strip of grass.
We would pull off the road onto that median and
pick dandelion. Mom would mix them with pork
and beans, hardboiled eggs, oil, and vinegar.
Joey

# CHAPTER 5
# HERSTORY, HISTORY

Sometimes before we would get started up on the bandstand,
I would say, "Now I'd like to introduce the band."
Then we would shake each other's hands.
Sam

I remember in high school telling mom to stay home
and answer the phone, "I love WAMS."
This local radio station was having a contest
and she actually won!!!
Tina

I remember our 1949 Plymouth,
at the time gas was 28¢/gallon.
I was wearing a white suit and tie.
Annie and I went out for a ride.
I stopped for gas and a soda. Well the soda vending
machine went wacky and money was pouring out
like a jackpot!
I also remember when gas stations were full service.
Attendants would wash car windows, check oil,
give green stamps and free drinking glasses.
Dad

I remember running errands on Saturday
to the bank or hardware store.
Dad opened the car window and rested his arm in
the L-shape with his fingers touching the top of the
window. I was wishing for the time
when I would be grown up and able to do that too.
Byron

All I remember about Portugal was going to the beach at midnight. There were eight of us and we snuck out of the hotel away from the chaperones. We took blankets from the hotel. The sky was so clear that night it was like a planetarium.
Linda A

Joey says he remembers Linda ran out of money and mom & dad had to wire her some. Also, the women in Portugal called her names because of her short skirt.
Joey, her brother

I remember when Cora was visiting and was ready to go shopping. She comes to the kitchen all dressed, with her purse and ready to go! I still had breakfast dishes to do, make the bed AND
I was still in my night gown!
Dina

I remember playing games at Yvette's aunt's house. In the parlor it was very nice and not for kids. Instead, we played in the laundry room where the floor was cold.
Lisa

Mary was checking car rental rates and found that Payless Car Rental had a good deal. Her dad
(who didn't know that Payless was a company name) thought that would be the case and said,
"Mary, why wouldn't you want to pay less!"
Lisa

At the time, we were attending St. John
the Beloved Church,
I remember Father DiMichael who knew us from
St. Matthew's Church wanted all of us Italians to go
to HIS new church at St. Mary of the Assumption.
It was 1956 and our relatives could not believe that
we wanted to move. My grandparents were getting
old; I was getting ready for college,
so we closed the Belvedere Sub Shop.
This was in Hockessin and our house did not even
have a number or a street name.
We would sit on the porch and see deer and fox.
Theresa


When Ben & Emily were younger, I would often be
in line at their school for drop-off and pick-up.
I noticed there was a couple with the same vehicle.
We called them Mr & Mrs Hummer.
Tony


I remember Alexander who painted churches and
altars helped me find the lot where we now live.
Alexander said to tell the current owner that you
liked how it was and wouldn't change it
(but of course we did).
It was like a jungle with vines you could swing on.
They were living like hobos with barely a path to
the entrance. Hopwell did sell us the lot for $5,000
and it took some work to clear it out!
Dad

Growing up, Joe was like a young scientist.
He ordered all kinds of things from catalogs.
The basement was filled
with flasks and beakers from his experiments.
Catherine

I don't remember ordering any flasks and beakers;
but I did order stuff from the
Edmund Scientific Catalog.
Joey

I remember one year, Joe made an igloo fort in our yard. He had soda trays or crates packed with snow.
I was amazed how warm it was inside.
Linda A

I remember making several forts but I don't remember one with soda crates. Usually Dad would pile up the snow from the driveway and sidewalk and I would tunnel in and hollow it out.
It was surprising how warm it was inside.
Joey

In high school, the sociology teacher wanted us to understand the concept of mores (pronounced morays). We were instructed to violate a typical social norm like taking money from church collection plate (instead of putting money in) and then write about.
It was winter and I wore my size 6 bikini to the Christiana Mall. Mom was a few steps behind and collected passer-by comments
that I could use for my assigned essay.
Lisa


In third grade at Marbrook Elementary, our teacher took us to the library during class. It was an atrium with the books in the center and classroom doors opened to this wide-open area. I was overwhelmed and had no idea how to choose a book. She directed me to biographies where I chose Clara Barton.
Even now, my favorite genre is memoir.
In high school, my teacher Sister Mary Edward gave me a template to keep track of books read.
**Since 1977, I have read over 5,000 books.**
I get many books from the Avondale Book Barn, local thrift stores and the dollar store. Another fun place is these Little Free Library book huts
found around town.
A few years ago, I signed up for Read Aloud Delaware. This organization pairs you up with a local daycare and you get to read one-on-one with the children. It's a very rewarding program for both the children and reader.
Lisa

## Memory of Yanko Cajnar by Barney Goodwin

I was a Western Cottage boarder from 1962-1964. Sunny Hills School (aka Sanford) was a wonderful place for an 8-year old who had just lost his mother to cancer. I remember sitting on a nail barrel in the woodshop getting a haircut. I remember watching Yanko remove a wall to expand Mrs. Wilson's 3rd grade classroom. I also remember him as Yanko, the cattleman.
In those years, Sanford had a beautiful herd of poled black Angus cattle roaming the schools' hilly pastures. As any big city boy who really wanted to be a farmer; in my own mind, I had "adopted" one of the herd, a large cow which I knew only as Number 12 for the chain around her neck and the brass pole tag numbered 12 which hung from it. I love cattle; I loved to hear them bellow on the hills behind Western in the morning; and I loved to get the Red Flyer wagon and go collect manure for the cottage garden.
I watched intently as Yanko cared for the herd. Once, he stopped and gently rebuked a few of us for damming up the creek in front of Western, carefully explaining to us that it would deprive the herd of water.
One afternoon there was a commotion over the hill behind the kindergarten building located next to Western. A cow was bellowing wildly.

One of the older Western boys came running down the hill describing a cow giving birth, but it was caught in the fence on the backside of the hill. Someone summoned Yanko who arrived with his son and the red and white tractor.

I was not allowed over the hill to observe. What I do remember was that Yanko and his son returned from the area of the old landfill further down the road from Western.

His son was standing, driving the tractor; while Yanko was sitting behind him, facing the rear with his chin in his hands, his elbows on his knees and a somber look on his face.

They had buried my Number 12.

That day, I saw the heart of the Sunny Hills Cattleman. He cared not only for the school he loved so much, the boys he taught and whose hair he cut; but also the cattle whose water source he protected and whose pastures he managed. The next day, I wandered into the white barn. There, hanging on a post, was the chain with the brass tag embossed with the large 12. I took it in my small hands, wanting to keep it. Empty handed, I left the barn carrying away memories that are still alive over 40 years later. These are fond memories of Yanko and Sunny Hills School which are rekindled with every Angus that I pass in the rolling pastures of Southern Ohio.

My name is Jaroslav Friedrich. I was born in Pistion near Litomerice on the river Labe. My mother was Czech, her name was Anna Levova. My stepfather's name was Rudolf Friedrich.

My name was Jaroslav Lev, but my mother married Mr. Rudolf Friedrich in 1934 and the name Friedrich was given to me before

I entered school in 1938; so my real father could not find me. I was searching for him and he was searching for me. I received the information from the Red Cross in 1970 which had been hidden by my stepfather. As soon as I had the address, I got on the train and found his place. His wife told me that his body is in the grave. Later my wife and I visited his wife and I could see a large photo on the wall of him.

I remember when I was 14 years old and rode my bike from Litomerice over the top of the mountain to Erzgebinge. One aunt had potatoes and sour cheese. I took half of these to another aunt in Decin and the other half I brought home.

This trip was forty-two kilometres one way!

Your name reminds me of the song "Mona Lisa" from my younger days. Mona Lisa, Mona Lisa, must have named you so like the lady with the mystic smile.

Is it only because you are lonely?

They have blamed you for that Mona Lisa strangeness in your smile. Do you smile to tempt lovers, Mona Lisa, or is this your way to hide a broken heart. Many dreams have been brought to your doorstep, they just lie there and they die there.

In 1945 money was not too important; barter was the means of exchange. I worked in a bakery and I took a roll to a pub to get a drink. A farmer would want shoes or cloth in return for food.
Many people would lament,
"The farmers are getting wealthy and their cows are standing on carpets!"

In August 1947 my mother and I went across the border from the German to the U.S. zone. We were captured on the road from Aš to Františkovy-Lázne. We were sentenced to 180 days for illegally crossing the border.

My brother Aaron plays rugby for the Wilmington Men's Club, but when he was just out of high school, he played for the 18-24 year old men's team, which allowed him to compete in tournaments around the world.  It's a BRUTAL sport, but he was quite good and agile.  He spent several weeks in both Auckland and Melbourne with some travel to other areas of each country to compete.  He also participated in tournaments in Belgium, France, England, Canada and Ireland, where he spent a whole semester studying at Trinity College while playing.  Actually, with his apartment being down the street from the Guinness Factory in Ireland, I don't know how much studying got done!  As he's gotten a little older, he has not traveled to other countries, but still plays for the Colts and plays in tournaments locally and in other close states.  When I go to see him play, I have absolutely NO IDEA what the hell I'm watching! It's like a mixture of soccer and football, but with NO protective gear.  I just clap when everyone else does and boo when everyone else does!
Chris


There are 12 years between Jean and I, so mom would have me take care of my little sister. One time, I went to play football and Jean was on the bleachers watching and waiting. Well, the mosquitoes really had a feast and boy, did her face show it! She had an allergic reaction to all those bites.
John C

My sister (author) booked my flight from Austin to
Philadelphia in which she upgraded me to first class
using frequent flyer points.
I was astonished by the gal next to me who opened
her compact and checked her make-up and lipstick
about a dozen times over that 3-hour flight.
Tony

❋

I remember going with my mom and my brother
Joseph to the Alamosa Sand Dunes.
Joseph ran WAY to the top while mom and I just
walked near the bottom of the "sand mountain."
Samantha

I remember going to the Colorado Alligator Farm.
I even got to hold a baby alligator.
Its mouth was taped shut so it wouldn't bite.
Joseph

❋

Grandpop Petrucci had a list on the door of the
house showing hours each kid had to be in,
according to age. One evening, John and Junior
were late due to working at the St Elizabeth carnival.
They knew they were past curfew so they slept
outside until Grandpop went to bed
and then they sneaked in.
Dorothy

When I was 7 years old, I went to Wilmington DE.
On the plane, I wore my favorite outfit: shorts and a tank top that were bright pink and purple.
Aunt Annie invited a few people over and made a lobster dinner. I was content with my peanut butter and jelly sandwich.
What in the world was I thinking!?
I remember Uncle Tony's amazing talent in carving wood ducks. He made me a beautiful one that I took home with me. It stayed on our mantlepiece for a long time.
Most of all, I remember the love that I felt when I was there. Someone took a photo of me holding a little flower in the front garden.
My mom put it in a little yellow frame and that remained on our refrigerator until I went to college. Aunt Annie and Uncle Tony filled me with some of the most wonderful memories of which I will always hold dear to my heart.
Jennifer

---

The kids disappeared after dinner when it was time to do the dishes.
But that was okay, they were doing their lessons.
It was a good time for my husband and I to talk.
He washed and I dried.
It was OUR time together.
Marion

I remember visiting family friends who lived on the
school grounds at Sanford.
There were not as many buildings there then.
We walked and played with the Cajnar sisters.
Tina

❃

October 2003, Oli from USAir took 10 of us to
Cancun. Diane and I went to an aquarium where
you could swim with the dolphins.
On this 3-day trip (before cell phone photos),
I took 7 rolls of film.
This was the most pictures that I had even taken
especially on such a short stay.
Lisa

❃

I was visiting my sister Mima. I filled my skirt with
figs from a tree near her apartment building.
Her husband Pero said he passed by there every day
and had never noticed the tree.
Another time, I visited Joey in California.
In his neighborhood, I was standing on the curb and
took a fig from a tree.
The owner saw me and shouted,
"Hey. Those are my figs!"
Catherine

After watching the movie based on the book
Bridges of Madison County
Matt wrote this poem:

*I should be sleeping*
*But I'm not*
*I just read a story*
*That won't be forgot*

*About covered bridges*
*And a woman*
*And I see myself*
*Or maybe just an omen*

*But the hunger and need*
*With its rhythmic passes*
*From which my inner life feeds*

*The wild orchids and the smell it made*
*That day in the Siskiyous*
*Was my Robert Kincaid.*

# CHAPTER 6
# HOLIDAYS

Ever peek inside a present and ruin the surprise?
Yes, I found a doll in my parent's closet that was supposed to be from Santa Claus. I knew it was mine since I was the only one at the time who would be playing with dolls.
When I mentioned it and looked again later,
it was gone.
Carol

Tracie had visited Santa Claus and was very concerned. She told her mother that they needed to buy some Scotch tape for Santa Claus.
Why?
"Cause Santa's eyebrow is falling off!"
Diana

I remember my first Christmas away from home.
My house seemed small since we were so used to a house full of people on Christmas and a lot of noise. Now with all the grandkids the house is full again and for sure a lot of noise,
I love it, even though I get tired.
My favorite Christmas tradition is making pizzelles. Everyone including my friends at work wait
for pizzelles at Christmas.
Linda A

One would think that after enjoying life for 80 years, the 80 Christmases would be in the forefront of one's memory.
They are not too vivid in mine; my courtship, marriage, births, children and grandchildren hold that honor.

During the depression of the 1930's, the searching for a tree in the woods stands out as does the paper we would cut to decorate it (color comic strips from old Sunday papers collected from neighbors) and our midnight mass church services as well as Christmas morning to get our gift of a box of clear toy candy - AND - the carols the nuns taught us.
WOW! WOW! WOW!

Now my memory jumps way ahead
to the late 1960's.
OH! What joy having two lovely daughters to see opening their presents: a typewriter for one, and Chatty Cathy doll for the other AND surprise after surprise causing breakfast to be delayed!
The excitement of getting together with our whole family and extended family on Christmas Day in these most recent years cannot be explained with words -- my heart rings with joy as loud as any church bells can toll - AND - I feel the Christ Child with us as surely did the three kings oh so long ago.

Charlie

I remember my daughter Kelly did not want to visit any Santa at local stores but she did come to the office where I worked. This guy let his beard grow out and had a Santa outfit on, so Kelly did see that guy. She told her dad that Santa was Bert Wood.
Mary H


I remember when I was at the age when I did not quite believe in Santa Claus anymore, I had found a great big doll in my mom's closet, so I knew she bought it. Later that night, someone showed up dressed in full-gear Santa outfit.
To this day, we still don't know who it was.
Carol

I remember the first shopping center in Wilmington, and I took Tina and Tony there to get their picture with Santa.
Dad


I remember the Carpenter's Union Labor Day parade and picnic; an all-day event with free food.
It was a highlight of our summer.
Tina

# CHAPTER 7
# LIBATIONS

I remember asking my sister-in-law Cindy what I should bring to her house for a family get-together. "Oh, your sweet tea, please!" Well, I would bring a big pitcher that was so heavy. I would carry it; and Zachary was young then, Malcolm carried him in the baby carrier.
Mary C

When I was younger, my grandmother brewed homemade beer in her kitchen which she served three times a day. Back then, we had four meals a day, so breakfast was the only time there was no beer served.
Charlie

One time, my mom wanted to drink Grasshoppers. She complained,
"Sonny, they didn't make this right."
I did not realize what a connoisseur she was.
We were at the Appalachian Inn and mom had gone to the restroom and was in there so long that I sent waitress in to check. She bombed out because she had been matching me drink for drink.
John C

I remember betting on racehorses with liquor names like Brandy, Whiskey and on gray horses too.
John C

After work, Cora would take off her shoes.
I would ask if she wanted a drink and it took awhile
for her to say, "Oh Sonny, don't mind if I do."
Then she would say,
"Sonny, you cut me a wee bit short."
She wanted 1.5-ounce right on the line!
John C

I remember having a blast in Cancun at Señor Frog's
Bar where they dumped the bartender out the
window into the water
since it was located on a pier!
They played the *Ghost Buster* theme song.
If you opened your mouth,
they would squirt vodka to you with a
huge ghost buster-like squirt gun.
I had this half watermelon filled with vodka and an
entire fruit salad! My husband was drinking
Budweiser at $6.00 a can until we realized that
Corona was only 1.00 each.
They considered Bud an imported beer...duh.
My hubby also won a contest for being the first one
to drain a baby bottle full of beer. First prize was a
t-shirt which he wore proudly for years and it made
me smile every time he wore it.
Mary H

I would pick up Barba Ive at the Edison Company
and we would go right to a bar.  He would have
a boilermaker, a beer and two shots.
I would order a ginger ale.
He would affectionately say, "Stara Baba."
(old lady)
Uncle John

Albina was "Nana" and she drank orange soda.
When Michael, Kevin and other grandkids
were thirsty,
they wanted Nana's juice.
Catherine

I remember my teacher would ask,
"Why are your ears so red?"
We didn't tell her that we drank rakija
(pronounced rah keeya)
in the morning before school to warm up.
Dad

Catherine wore a hat with a "net."  This veil got in
the way since I wanted to kiss her.  I remember us
sitting in a booth sharing an ice cream soda – same
glass with two straws.
Uncle John

My buddy Pierce worked in the commissary.
He used gallons of canned apricots, canned peaches
and a blow torch to make just ONE PINT of
applejack whiskey with his still.
Uncle John

At a holiday party, I asked my niece Tina (the usual bartender) to mix some drinks. The rakija (Croatian alcoholic drink) was in a two-liter ginger ale bottle. So instead of making a "high ball,"
she was mixing moonshine with whisky.
Uncle John

※ ※

I remember my dad and Uncle Tony in the basement at the Lynam Street house where they were making wine.
It seems like they have had fifty years to perfect their wine-making skills and it should taste like Mogen David by now!
Linda A

※ ※

Barba Ive was a strong guy. He opened (and drank) twenty-five cans of beer; he took the bottle caps off with his teeth. One time he picked up Tony and me and lifted us up, one on each arm.
Uncle John

## CHAPTER 8
## LIFE LESSONS

My mom used to say,
"If your feet feel good, you feel good all over."
Kim

I remember my dad would ask,
"What size shoe do you wear?"
I would say, "Seven."
He would then reply, "Stand upon it."
This means, life is not fair so don't use any
circumstances to excuse the problem;
just keep on going.
Nancy

I remember when we were little and accidentally
dropped our lollipop,
but of course we still wanted to eat it.
So we sang this little song and then it was okay,
"God made dirt;
dirt doesn't hurt,
kiss it up to God and let the dirt go to work."
Liz

I remember my friend Lolly painted her living room
a color called "Mother of God Blue."
Linda M

If I had poison ivy or another ailment,
my dad would say, "Go jump in the ocean,
because salt water cures everything."
Eleanor

My mom used to say: Mankaio ne sacho
(What do I know?)
Mom

I remember driving in the car with Barba Ive.
If there was a girl wearing shorts too short,
he would say, "Vrajži Americanske ženske."
Joey

There's an old saying, "There's old pilots and there's
bold pilots but there's few old bold pilots,
or no old bold pilots."
Melody

My friend Ann's dad and my dad's favorite saying,
"Bambina Madonna."
Translation: Oh my gosh!
Etta

## 2 from Linda A
I remember Nani's white china cabinet where she
kept the wine and other liquors.  She would take
them out, one at a time and say,
"Here try this, or this one."

I remember Uncle Emil's favorite saying,
"How sweet it is."
I remember his wife, Albina,
would drive at night with sunglasses on.
I also remember going fishing at Augustine Beach
with Uncle Emil, Aunt Albina and my cousins.

## Many from Dad

Childhood song: Tony Baloni che vende limoni in piazza Goldoni
3 apri la pozto e spande caffe

Dad tells his buddy that the best way to polish the accordion is with a diaper.
A clean one, of course!

There are more days than kielbasa!

When Boškin was hunting, he would say,
"Da ni pas se ferma za pišat onda nebi mu be zec pobega."
(If the dog did not stop to pee,
the rabbit would not get away).

I remember a small mouse puppet
on the Ed Sullivan called Toppo Gigio.
A frequent phrase was "shut the door."
One time recently I was imitating him and said,
"Shut the door." My daughter Tina looked around
and said, "What? The door is shut!"

I remember my boss, Sam DeMauro would say,
"Take the good with the bad" and
"Better half a loaf of bread than none."

I remember a foreman named Alan
who constantly said,
"Excuse me for breathing."

## 2 from Rosina

Let me tell you about my grandchildren Nikola, the big sister, will caress her little brother Anthony on the face and cheek. Then jealousy makes a visit and in the next moment, she pushes him. Now he's getting a little bigger, and he has strength and will pull her hair. Ohhhhh, she does not like that!

All over the world there are good and bad people
Some may give their shirt off their back;
others want to take your shirt and your skin

∞   ∞

## 4 from Sam
Do you know "Play by the Door"?
(I'll help you out!)

Are you taking requests?
Do you know "Go Home"?

I'll never forget what's his name.

On the map, one inch = 100 feet. Sam remembers working with Charlie who would point to the surveyor map and his thumb was so big he would cover 300 feet!

## Author Bon Mots

Heaven's gonna be better than this.

The answer is no, unless you ask.

Just because you're thin or wealthy,
doesn't mean you're happy or healthy.

Overheard conversation:
Someone: How are you?
Lisa: Super dooper!

Another encounter:
Why do you walk backwards down the stairs?
Lisa: I've heard there's less chance of falling,
and it's better for your knees.

From a children's book in which the gardener
wanted to keep out children. She had a sign,
"Beware of the pyracantha."
Which sounds ominous, but it's just a plant.

"We live in the hearts of those we leave behind."
As a teenager, I went on a few Christian spiritual
retreats, usually on the weekends. This quote was in
a movie we watched at one of those events.

Kittens can have milk.
Once they are grown,
most cats are lactose-intolerant
and should have water not milk!

When I would run errands with Dad, even when the car was not so new anymore, I would park far from store entrance. He would say,
"Why don't you just park at home?!"
If he waited in the car while I ran inside the store,
I would return and say,
"Thanks for waiting."
Dad's reply, "Did I have a choice?"
Lisa

Exasperated by a life or work situation, Cindy says,
"You just can't write this stuff."

Happy about a good bargain, Mom would say,
"I made out like a bandit."

I had a female flight instructor that basically told me, don't believe everything that someone else tells you about yourself.
Melody

My dad would visit his sister Catherine almost every day. She had a neighbor who would come home from work around 6pm and stop in to visit. Eventually, they would save him some dinner. He seemed to have an endless appetite, so my dad nicknamed him "Mangia Tutto."
In Italian, this means "eat everything."
Lisa

# CHAPTER 9
# PILOTS

## Chapter 9 notes

These stories are from commercial airline pilots based on interviews for my doctoral dissertation:

*How do female airline pilots experience and describe achieving their career goals.*

**Author's note: This document is available on Google Scholar**

You may have noticed schools encouraging more coursework in STEM education
(science, technology, engineering and mathematics),
especially for girls.
Let's include aviation and STEAM ahead !

It's important to have some female pilots go out to do career day talks. I remember approaching one of the girls. She was in awe, a little bit.
I asked, "Do you want to be a pilot someday."
(I was thinking, oh boy, I'm gonna plant the seed in this little girl's head." I did not expect her reply, "No, I want to be an astronaut!"
Rachel

¤   ¤

I have a lot of people say, "Oh what do you do for a living?" I'm a pilot. Oh, you mean a flight attendant. Nooooooo I mean a pilot. I'm not so stupid that I don't know what I do for my job.
Felicity

¤   ¤

I kinda set people up because I think it's comical. They go, "What do you do? Where do you work?"
"Oh, I work at the airport."
"Oh, you're a flight attendant?"
No, I'm a pilot.
You can tell what the outcome is gonna be before we even start down that path because I can tell that they're locked in the mentality of "if you're a girl, you're a flight attendant."
Bonnie

About 20 years ago I was flying for the commuter airlines which didn't have a flight attendant.
The plane was small enough that it had 19 passengers, the pilot and co-pilot. One lady came up and chewed me out. She growled, "What's wrong?! You were up there flirting with the pilot the whole time and you never came back here and offered us anything to drink." Oh really, here's my employee number, here's my boss's phone number,
you call my boss and tell him what I was doing,
are you kidding?
Bonnie

Another funny story, I had a door light come on in the back there in the airplane and so I got out of the cockpit and went back there to check the door.
And I'm in my uniform!
I was walking by and a guy grabbed my arm and he said, when you get back, I'd like a gin and tonic.
I said, "You and me both, buddy."
Bonnie

One of the other things that I just love in the Midwest when it's winter and there's cloudy days, foggy days, and you basically spend an hour de-icing and then you take-off and a thousand feet, two thousand feet, you break through the clouds, oh my goodness, there's the sun!
I love just sitting there in the sun, and looking down at the clouds, and remembering what it looked like from the other side.
Melody

Once I was going through security to Japan and my friend, another female pilot was having her birthday. So I brought a wine opener because in Japan we were gonna celebrate and have a bottle of wine. And this was well before all this TSA baloney. They took the wine opener away from me at the TSA checkpoint. And I'm standing there in uniform, so what's going on with that, why are you taking that away? And they held it up and they said, well, you might use it to get control of the aircraft. I gestured at my uniform, I said, "Really, I already have control of the aircraft."
Oh okay, keep the wine opener.
Bonnie

My stepsister and I had a discussion about me being a captain. She asked what's the hardest thing about being a captain that's different? I replied that on most airplanes the captain is the person that steers on the ground, all the time, and I would say that can be challenging. You have a little map and it's small and at my age, I need my glasses, you gotta have the light right, to be able to read this chart, and every taxiway is labeled like A (alpha) and you might get this read back that says turn right on yankee and hold short on Whiskey 10 and it goes on and on and you gotta write it down and follow the instructions and it's not so hard if you're familiar with the airport but it's hard if you're not. Of course the co-pilot can help you but in the end, if you make a mistake, it's your fault.
Melody

Especially early on, I was discouraged. I had this one male instructor for flying that basically thought this wasn't a good idea. Conversely, my next instructor got out of the airplane ready to solo me.
I exclaimed, NO, I'm not going by myself.
He explained, well, you gotta go by yourself eventually, so what's wrong with today.
Melody

My uncle called up my parents one day and said, Oh, I'm gonna take the airplane out. Do you think Felicity would want to come. He was a pilot, just a recreational pilot, on his own, not for an airline or anything, and he'd been a mechanic back in the 70s for United and so he'd been around aviation for a very long time, probably about 20 years at that point. So we went out flying. He had skis out on his airplane, being from Northern MN, he took me up to a frozen lake by the house.
His daughter was in the plane, she was 8, and she was screaming her lungs off the whole time,
"I hate this. Take me down." Just freaking out.
And I'm looking out the window, this is really cool.
I think I want to do this when I grow up. It wasn't like I want to do this as a job, I just thought, oh I would want to learn how to fly when I grow up. And as the years went on, eventually, I thought oh, I think I'll do this as a job. Yes, he's the one that got me interested in flying.
Felicity

I went through private, commercial, instrument and instructor training within 3 years. That's a lot to get done in 3 years. I was really clear with any guy that I dated, either you get on board
or get out of the way.
Angela

Before I officially decided on college, my mom and dad, said, ya know before you do this, you should maybe decide, and they knew that I hadn't been on a plane very often, you should maybe decide if you really want to do it. For my 16th birthday they gave me half the money to go get some introductory lessons and the other half I earned with my job. They said, go get these lessons and if you decide you want to go do this then we're gonna go look at colleges. I did that. I said, yep, this is great. I still want to do this. So that's when we went and looked at the Univ of ND which is only about 4 hours away from home. I actually wanted to go to Univ of FLA that also had a campus in AZ. I said, "Dad, what about one of those?" He was kind of freaked out that is was too far away from home. Go to UND and if you hate UND then we can have a conversation. I went to UND, I went on the coldest day of the year. I went in the middle of January, I don't even know why, middle of January, not even exaggerating, it was like 15 below that day. And I still came away, yup I want to go to this school, I want to go today, I don't want to finish high school. I just want to go.
Felicity

I was on vacation one time in Hawaii, we were in a helicopter looking at one of the volcanoes and I got to talking with the helicopter pilot, the family that I was on board with us said, "Oh you're a pilot?"
They had a teenage daughter with them, and I started talking to her about it. And I said, oh yea, you can do this and you can do that. And her grandmother, "Or honey, you could be a flight attendant." And I looked at the grandmother and said, "Or she could be a pilot."
A great story actually that my friend just told me, she was talking to her friend's son, and her friend is a pilot as well. "Oh, do you want to be a pilot when you grow up, like your mom?" And the little boy said, "No, that's a girl's job."
That was awesome, the best thing that I heard. We're getting somewhere finally.
Felicity

In 2004, I was on a connecting flight in Miami. There was a little boy about 10 years old near my partner Ryan. He said, "I know the captain, do you want to meet him?"
At the time, I was in civilian clothes.
Ryan said, "Jenna is a pilot too."
In his proper British accent we heard, "That's impossible, everyone knows girls can't fly planes."
And he was so matter of fact about this.
I was so surprised by his conviction.
How was that little boy so certain!?
Jenna

I like to stand and say bye to the passengers.
One because half the time the other guy's just on his phone,
checking his messages. So I feel like someone should do it.
I hate it when the pilots are just up there
and they don't talk to anyone.
Two because a little part of me wants to be visible,
I feel I owe that. Not to be feminist roar, but I feel like being
a little bit more visible, maybe there is some girl that's gonna
walk by and say, "I didn't know girls can be pilots,
that's so awesome."
Claudia

It's a stressful job. You're away from home a lot. You're gone
3 days at a time, some are 4 days.
And it's never on the same schedule, it's not every Mon-Tues-
Wed, the next week you're Fri-Sat-Sun. You can't take night
classes, you can't go back to school, you can't be there for a
monthly book club on Thursday. It's a real hole in your life.
Rose

I was number 3 in FO in ACY (first officer in Atlantic City)
where I'm based, I'm now 36 of 37 in captain. I get no days
off that I want, I get nothing.
But it's ok because my husband does not get them off either.
He just started at Jet Blue, so we just decided we're gonna
move the holidays around to suit ourselves.
Claudia

Someone once told me when I was first starting,
"Take the first (commercial pilot) job that you can get,
just to get locked into your seniority."
I think that was terrible advice and I'm really glad
that I didn't listen to it.
Claudia

It was my maternal grandmother Lydia who funded my college education. She was the one who really made a leap of faith to believe the endeavor was worth her money. She was my first passenger. She was born in 1900 before the first flight. The only concern I ever heard her express was if I would be flying at Piedmont with a man - not because she thought it was a man's job, but because she thought it was always nice to have a man around to do the heavy work. She also expressed disappointment in our manly uniforms as she always wore dresses or skirts, never slacks.

Rose

I really could have been captain 6 months ago. I was like, hmmm, it was that imposter symptom kicking in.

As pilot in command of an aircraft, the buck stops here, so you have to be comfortable with being that person and that's another thing that I find that's hard as a girl. There's an article about imposter's syndrome. It's all professions and it's like a female thing, you feel like you have to prove yourself 18x harder than anyone else. They talked about it specifically for women in the science fields. They can go in there and have straight A's in undergrad, straight A's in grad school, and they still get their doctoral thesis and they think that they don't belong, that they're not worthy of the sort of praise that they're getting.

Claudia

When I was in school, I started to take an aviation class in 10th grade. And it was because I was in the band, and the band director was always late.
I knew to have peace at home, I would have to do something different.
I chose an aeronautics class. It was the first time they offered it. From that, it got me into a flying club at the local airport. Almost every 3 months, they gave someone a solo for free. If you do really well on a basic aviation class, and I was a really good student, so I got to do my solo for free. And really it was supposed to be the Young Bucks Flying Club
but I showed up, they did not know what to do so they just let me stay. But it worked out for me, because I got to solo and I got a job at the airport that paid for up to my private pilot's license while I was in high school.
It was fate.
The Young Buck's Flying Club had gotten this money from the Optimist's Club, they were trying to get wayward boys to get into something other than graffiti. But it helped me immensely. It was this fateful thing. There was a lot of fate that happened, like the band director was chronically late,
my mother had one car and 5 children. There was no way that she could sit around and wait for me. So it got me into the aeronautics class. I don't know how my aviation career would have moved forward without these people and influences…all because the band director had been late.
Rose

If a guy has a bad landing, it's just because he had a
bad day. If a gal has a bad landing, it's because she's
female and can't fly. You still get that sort of stigma.
Even now, the discrimination can be subtle.
As a woman, you can feel isolated.
If a woman really wants to do this and loves it,
she's gonna find support from family or somebody.
She'll succeed.
If she's just a little tentative, or a little unsure,
it's gonna be tougher to pursue an aviation career.
Jenna


I sat down in the cockpit one time and this guy looks
across from me. He just came in and said hi and sat
down. He didn't say much for a minute or two.
Then he looked over at me and finally said,
"Oh, I suppose I should tell you, I'm of the opinion
that women shouldn't be allowed to drive."
I replied, "And even more so that women shouldn't
be allowed in cockpits of airplanes, right?"
He looked at me and smirked,
"Something like that."
I said, "Ok, good to know where you're coming from."
And I continued to do my job and said,
"Ready for the checklist?"
I think he was waiting for me to be mad.
In my opinion, if you are professional then you do
your job just like anyone else and don't make a big
deal over the fact that you're a minority gender.
Rachel

# CHAPTER 10
# TRAVEL AGENTS

I remember filling out forms for ticket exchanges.
In travel agent lingo they are called RENs
(Refund Exchange Notice).
Instead of whiteout to cover any errors, since the RENs were green, I had "green out."
Mary H

I was booking a flight for my client Louis.
He mentioned that he knew Lisa (the author) as their families were close. He said he remembered changing her diaper! At the time, she was 28 and a bit embarrassed by this revelation.
Cathy

My first FAM trip was to Sandals All-Inclusive Resort in Nassau. Three days for $50.
I spent one entire day sitting at the pool bar.
Mandy

I won free first-class tickets on American Airlines when I worked at Rosenbluth Travel Agency.
We decided to go to Las Vegas and had to connect in Dallas both directions. On one of the flights a lady had a tropical fish in a plastic bag and the stewardess wouldn't let her keep it in the cabin so she put it in the overhead and kept opening it up to check on it. We also had a rack of horns on the flight but they were in coach so I cannot verify that one.
Mary H

## Travel Memories from Lisa

I remember one FAM trip to Tokyo on All Nippon Airlines for $125.00. We flew business class and stayed in a hotel which had mirrors that did not get fogged up when taking a shower. This hotel was also operated by ANA, so we could checkin for our flight and check our bags in the hotel lobby!

At least once a year, I go to the Nashville area to visit family. When I'm there we are a dozen cousins. When I visit San Jose, we are half a dozen!

The most expensive airline ticket that I ever booked was first class from Philadelphia to Sydney for $25,000.
Eventually this traveler flew three times!

After high school, my mom and dad helped plan six weeks in Paris where I could take classes at the American International College. One class was Sociology. The other was Art History which included trips to many of the local French museums.
My favorite was Claude Monet's garden at Giverny.

I was surprised the first time, but after that, the travel request became a common occurrence. As a matter of fact, it still amazes me to hear, "I need a flight to Barcelona ---
departing tomorrow !"

Notes from my most recent trip Down Under (SEP 2023).
In New Zealand, they pronounce the "z" like "zed."
So I went to N.Zed and drove on the other side of the road from Auckland to Wellington in the North Island. Short flight. Then drove Christchurch to Queenstown on the South Island.
It was spring and the mountains still had snow.
The landscape was beautiful.
I drove hundreds of miles past many farms.

At one hotel, there was a dessert called banoffee.
I was intrigued but did not want a full slice.
At one table was a boy and his father. So I asked the waitress to cut the cheesecake and serve it on two plates and gave one plate to them.

While driving, there would be a sign to discourage traffic. As I was usually the slow driver eager to see every sight and take pictures, I thought that was a great idea, however many times there was no place to pull over!

I was lucky to stay in one 4-star hotel in Auckland but I was disappointed that the phone did not work and the lever to open/close the curtain broke. I was impressed by the shower that had two heads, one for someone my height, another for someone 6' tall.

Did you know...they have few banks in NZ?
Most people use credit cards and the ATM.
So many places there do not have
any physical bank building.

My colleague Sisina told me about a traveler
who requested flights for Dayton
(Ohio, airport code DAY) but was booked for
Daytona Beach (FLA, airport code DAB).
Scooby Doo says, "Rut roh."

In the fall of 1993, I was at work and ready to send
a fax just as there was an incoming page which
described a travel agent familiarization trip (FAM)
to Greece for $250. This price included airfare,
hotels, some meals and a Santorini day cruise.
As the trip was limited to the first ten who paid,
you can be sure that I did not share this with anyone
else in the office and quickly sent my check.

I took a trip to Kenosha, Wisconsin. There was a
hotel in which you could have one of their cats in
your room (with food, water, litter box).
My cat was Romeo.
They delivered him to my room, and he just slept on
the bed. I unpacked a few things from my suitcase
and organized items for the next day. Finally,
around 11pm, I go to bed. About 2 hours later,
Romeo decided it was time to play.
I was not a fan of that idea!

A traveler was booking flights from Seattle to Tampa
for a training class. He decided to add an extra day
and visit his brother. Before departure, he called
with the news and found out that his brother had
moved back to the West Coast!

On one trip to Canada with my friends Caroline & Don, we stayed in a cabin. The front desk gal gave us our key and said, "You're in my favorite cabin!" We were still in the lobby / gift shop area and heard her say the same thing to the next people who were checking in!
The next morning, Don ran the shower for over 20 minutes before there was hot water.
On this trip we stayed at a hotel near Banff and walked about 10 miles to get to the Paint Pots. These are colorful pools of mineral water.
I got a head start on this hike, and along the way dropped little notes for them.

When I first started working as a travel agent, many hotels offered a 50% discount.
At a Days Inn in the Shenandoah area, the room rate was $28, which meant that I only paid $14.
A few years after that, one hotel chain had a travel discount where rooms were $35/night.
I stayed in a New York City hotel for that amazingly low price.

One of the most expensive hotel nights ($269) was in Hershey PA when cousin Carol and I stayed to be close to the Dancing with the Stars venue.
The key card lock did not work and we had to get front desk help several times. We should have asked the manager on duty for a upfront room discount, but she only offered 50% off on our next stay.
We never went back.

One trip with cousin Carol, we were lucky to stay two nights at the Nemacolin Resort.
We were upgraded to a junior suite which had a huge dining table, living room, two bedrooms.
The French doors had a view of the hotel landscaping and the iconic Nemacolin sign.
One of their attractions was a TINY House.
I also did the zipline there.

Trying to cover all 50 states, in one week I traveled to Minnesota, Iowa, Nebraska, Kansas and South Dakota, legitimately called my MINKS trip.

On a FAM trip to NYC there were several agents and we were hosted by different hotels and Amtrak. At one restaurant we had a buffet delivered to our table. The appetizers were so lavish and unusual (like quinoa), it was surprising we had room for dinner. It was the first time that I had lunch in a Bento box.

I'm often asked if I like to take a cruise.
Yes, but not on your typical itinerary, instead
Galapagos Islands cruise
Cruise the Nile
Cruise down Norway's coast (fjords)
Cruise from Argentina to Antarctica, part of our cruise was Drake Lake and part was a humbling Drake Shake
Once I heard the name "Tierra del Fuego," I knew that I had to go!

## Reasons That I've Traveled

To go to rhyming cities like Boston & Austin
To go to exotic places like Rio then Reno
And to island countries like Iceland and Ireland
And smaller places like Smith Island for their
traditional 8 to 10-layer cake

<u>Waterfalls!</u>
Niagara Falls, Victoria Falls, and Iguazu Falls

<u>Mountains</u>
Colorado & Canadian Rockies and the Swiss Alps

Inside too – like the Corkscrew Canyon in Page AZ
A picture of this canyon was on the cover
of a college textbook.
Eventually I traveled out west for this scenic treasure.

<u>Hot air balloon festivals</u>
Albuquerque International Balloon Fiesta
Des Moines Balloon Classic
Festival of Ballooning in Flemington NJ
Glen Falls Balloon Fest
Pocono Balloon Fest
Red Rock Balloon Rally

I wish for you …. Travel memories too!
I am planning less trips these days, but look forward to one final
European trek with Emily to see:
Our friend Lauren in Paris
Our cousin Jennifer in Dunboyne, and
Our cousin Ksenija in Rome.

# Appendix

Here is a list of some favorite authors
and supplemental notes

Advice from a recent tome about the Latte Factor:

The author recommended having $5 a day deducted from paycheck, so that's about $100/month.
Ask your employer to have this deduction deposited to your account that is not easily accessed and accrues interest.
When ready to retire in 30 years,
you could have close to a million.

## Notes related to appendix

My friend Chris Scopazzi was taking a trip to Germany and he wanted to borrow the travel guide that I had. I agreed if he in turn let me have one of his books which turned out to be by P.G. Wodehouse. I don't read many novels but decided to read the book in our exchange and I loved it.
It's a trifecta of humor, plot twists
and lovable characters.
Now I have more than half of PGW's
90 books in my library.
When out at a restaurant, I remember Chris would only eat half his dinner to save room for dessert!

My newest interest is adult graphic novels.
I have read several by Roz Chast including her book on NYC and another on dealing with aging parents.

Just before that, I had found a junior adult graphic called Real Friends by Shannon Hale
about the trials of mean girls, bullies,
and life in elementary school

Another favorite are visual journals like
When Wanderers Cease to Roam
by Vivian Swift -and-
Little Things in a Big Country
by Hannah Hinchman

In the list on the following pages,
** denotes that this author has many more good books !

Armstrong, Karen
Through the Narrow Gate

Ayers, Pam
You Made Me Late Again!

Brand, Paul and Phil Yancey
Fearfully and Wonderfully Made

Brilliant, Ashleigh **
I'm Just Moving Clouds Today

Brown, Brené **
Atlas of the Heart

Buscaglia, Leo **
Bus 9 to Paradise

Cain, Susan
Quiet Power

Canfield, Jack and Mark Hansen
The Aladdin Factor

Crosley, Sloane
I Was Told There'd Be Cake

de Mello, Anthony
Awareness

Eichenreich, Barbara **
Solace of Open Space

Fuller, Alexandra **
Scribbling the Cat

Fulwiler, Jennifer **
One Beautiful Dream

Gladwell, Malcolm **
Blink; Outliers

Goldberg, Natalie
Writing Down the Bones

Halliday, Ayun
No Touch Monkey!

Hansen, Mark and Barbara Nichols
Out of the Blue

Hatmaker, Jen **
Of Mess and Moxie

Kennedy, Susan Ariel Rainbow (SARK) **
Inspiration Sandwich

Kephart, Beth
Handling the Truth

Keyes, Marian
Under the Duvet

Kingsolver, Barbara
High Tide in Tuscon

Klam, Julie
Friendkeeping

Kübler-Ross, Elisabeth **
Wheel of Life
Did you know she was one of triplets?
And did you know ... she is misquoted many times
for her seminal work on grief.
It's stages of <u>dying</u> – not stages of <u>grieving</u>.

Lamott, Anne **
Help, Thanks, Wow

L'engle, Madeleine **
A Circle of Quiet

Lindbergh, Anne Morrow
**My all-time favorite: Gift from the Sea**

Markham, Beryl
West With the Night

Miller, Donald
Blue Like Jazz

Morris, Mary
Nothing to Declare

Niequist, Shauna
Bittersweet

O'Brien, Stacey
Wesley the Owl

Orlean, Susan
My Kind of Place

Pipher, Mary **
Another Country

Remen, Rachel Naomi
Kitchen Table Wisdom

Renfroe, Anita
Everything – books and especially DVDs
Find her MOM song online
Elvira Gallego sings The Child Song in reply
Renfroe also has DAD and Grandma songs – all fun

Roach, Mary **
Gulp

Rosenthal, Amy **
The Book of Eleven

Sacks, Oliver **
Gratitude

Salter, James & Kay
Life is Meals

Scottoline, Lisa
Why My Third Husband Will Be a Dog

Shankle, Rachel **
Sparkly Green Earrings

Siegel, Bernie
Love, Medicine & Miracles

TerKeurst, Lysa **
The Best Yes

Trillin, Calvin **
Travels with Alice

Truss, Lynne
Talk to the Hand

Wise, Nina
A Big New Happy Unusual Life

Wyse, Lois
Funny, You Don't Look Like a Grandmother

**\*\* Denotes that this author has many more good books**

## Favorite Kid Books

Baker, Keith
Little Green Peas

Bruel, Nick
Bad Kitty series

DiCamillo, Kate
La La La

Eastman, P.D.
Go, Dog, Go!

Harper, Charise
Just Grace series

Lansky, Bruce
A Bad Case of the Giggles

McCarty, Peter
Fabian Escapes

Nystrom, Marty
Don't Mess with Moses!

Prelutsky, Jack
The New Kid on the Block

Schade, Susan and Jon Buller
Snow Bugs

Scotton, Rob
Splat the Cat

Silverstein, Shel
Falling Up

# Index

| Adelaide | Food secret | 14 |
|---|---|---|
| Angela | Get on board | 61 |
| Barney | Yanko Cajnar | 30 |
|  | Number 12 | 31 |
| Ben | Fishing | 10 |
| Bonnie | Work at the airport | 57 |
|  | Commuter flight | 58 |
|  | Gin and tonic | 58 |
|  | Wine opener | 59 |
| Byron | Tipped canoe | 7 |
|  | Hero | 25 |
| Carol | Wedding cookies | 4 |
|  | Secret doll | 40 |
|  | Anonymous Santa | 42 |
| Catherine | Blueberry pie | 13 |
|  | Science experiment | 28 |
|  | Figs | 37 |
|  | Nana's juice | 46 |
| Cathy | Louis' secret | 68 |
| Charlie | Christmas memories | 41 |
|  | Grandmother's brew | 44 |
| Chris | Aaron | 34 |
| Claudia | Feminist roar | 63 |
|  | Holidays | 63 |
|  | Seniority | 63 |
|  | Imposter syndrome | 64 |
| Dad | Bunny dinner | 2 |
|  | Childhood bounty | 14 |
|  | Northeast Yacht Club | 15 |
|  | Tomato titans | 17 |
|  | Soda machine jackpot | 25 |
|  | Wilmington jungle | 27 |
|  | Santa picture | 42 |
|  | Croatian moonshine | 46 |
| Denise B | Joy ride with Grandpa | 3 |
| Denise D | Babysitting big sister | 3 |

| | | |
|---|---|---|
| Denise M | Young mom | 2 |
| Diana | Santa's eyebrow | 40 |
| Dina | Cora's visit | 26 |
| Dorothy | Curfew | 35 |
| Dot | Apple soup | 16 |
| Eleanor | Beer and pretzels | 19 |
| Etta | Flour sack dress | 20 |
| Felicity | Not a flight attendant | 57 |
| | Ski plane | 60 |
| | Aviation bug | 61 |
| | Helicopter pilot | 62 |
| Feručo | Sailing vacation | 9 |
| Jaroslav | Childhood memories | 32-33 |
| Jean | Aunt Mary | 20 |
| Jenna | Girls can't fly planes | 62 |
| | Bad landing | 66 |
| Jennifer | DE memories | 36 |
| JoAnn | Flower girl princess | 4 |
| Joe B | Bananas flambé | 16 |
| | Barbara Ann | 17 |
| Joey | Fishing | 8 |
| | Capsized | 11 |
| | Dandelion delight | 23 |
| | Portugal | 26 |
| | Edmund Scientific | 28 |
| | Igloo fort | 28 |
| John C | Mosquito feast | 34 |
| | Grasshoppers | 44 |
| | Racehorses | 44 |
| | Cora after work | 45 |
| Joseph | Alligator farm | 35 |
| Judie | Ring ravioli | 15 |
| Larry | Guacamole | 17 |
| Linda A | Movie treats | 14 |
| | Portugal | 26 |
| | Igloo fort | 28 |
| | Pizzelles | 40 |
| | Mogen David | 47 |
| Linda M | Sweet fajitas | 19 |

| | | |
|---|---|---|
| Lisa | Baby Emily | 2 |
| | Baby Amelia | 2 |
| | Rainbow bridal party | 5 |
| | At the reception | 5 |
| | Birthday cake | 20 |
| | Yvette's aunt | 26 |
| | Pay less! | 26 |
| | Sociology experiment | 29 |
| | Clara Barton | 29 |
| | Cancun | 37 |
| | Mangia Tutto | 54 |
| | Travel memories | 69 |
| | New Zealand | 70 |
| | More travel memories | 71-74 |
| Mandy | FAM trip | 68 |
| Marion | Washing dishes | 36 |
| Mary C | Sweet tea | 44 |
| Mary H | Home garden | 22 |
| | Bert Wood Santa | 42 |
| | Senor Frog | 45 |
| | Green out | 68 |
| | Tropical fish | 68 |
| Matt | Siskiyou poem | 38 |
| Melody | Cloudy day | 58 |
| | Whiskey 10 | 59 |
| | Solo | 60 |
| Mitzi | Food memory | 16 |
| Mom | Croatian crepe | 17 |
| Nancy | Lesa and egg | 15 |
| Natalia | Pasta vongole | 13 |
| Natalie | Indian wedding | 4 |
| Pat | Onion snow | 23 |
| Peg | Mackerel breakfast | 13 |
| Rachel | Astronaut | 57 |
| | Follow checklist | 66 |
| Richard | Wild asparagus | 23 |
| Rose | No book club | 63 |
| | Lydia | 64 |
| | Young Buck's Flying Club | 65 |

| Sam | Bunny hop | 2 |
|---|---|---|
| | Polka ban | 4 |
| | Italian cat | 19 |
| | Band introduction | 25 |
| Samantha | Alamosa sand dunes | 35 |
| Sylvia | Russian dressing | 13 |
| Thelma | Italian grocer | 23 |
| Theresa | Hockessin | 27 |
| Tina | Mother's helper | 3 |
| | Wedding day | 5 |
| | Many memories | 18 |
| | Corky's slice | 19 |
| | I love WAMS | 25 |
| | Labor Day parade | 42 |
| | Cajnar sisters | 37 |
| Tony | Cali strawberries | 15 |
| | Mr & Mrs Hummer | 27 |
| | First class | 35 |
| Uncle John | Barba Ive | 7 |
| | The Kelly kids | 7 |
| | Bodega Bay | 7 |
| | Shark got away | 8 |
| | Mackerel fishing | 9 |
| | Indian River fishing | 10 |
| | Stara Baba | 46 |
| | Cream soda | 46 |
| | Applejack whiskey | 46 |
| | High ball | 47 |
| | Barba Ive | 47 |
| Venus | Babysitting travel | 2 |
| | Fortune cookie | 5 |

| Index for Chapter 8 | Life Lessons |
|---|---|
| Kim, Nancy, Liz, Linda M, Eleanor | 49 |
| Mom, Joey, Melody, Etta, Linda A | 50 |
| Dad | 51 |
| Rosina, Sam | 52 |
| Lisa | 53 |
| Lisa, Cindy, Mom, Melody | 54 |

Other works by Lisa Cristofich:

Newsletter editor
Signal Corps Association
1992-2004

Dina's Diary
1973 summer trip
2005

Newsletter editor
Delaware Accordion Club
2008 – 2024

Memories of Old West Annville
June 2010

Kittens, Kisses and Cousins
March 2024

## Prayers and Final Thoughts

The LORD bless you and keep you;
the LORD make his face shine on you and be gracious to you;
the LORD turn his face toward you and give you peace.

**Numbers 6: 24-26**

♥  ♥

And I pray that you, being rooted and established in love, may have power, together with all the Lord's holy people, to grasp how wide and long and high and deep is the love of Christ, and to know this love that surpasses knowledge—that you may be filled to the measure of all the fullness of God.

**Ephesians 3:17-19**

♥  ♥

O Lord, in the morning you hear my voice
In the morning I plead my case to you and wait.

**Psalms 5:3**

## ABOUT THE AUTHOR

For over 25 years, Lisa has worked in corporate travel. During this time, she traveled to all 50 states, 15 islands, 35 countries, and all 7 continents.
She always returns home to Delaware.
Her favorite pastime is BCC: book, cat, couch.
Since 1977, she has read over 5,000 books.

Made in the USA
Columbia, SC
01 May 2024

dd6f239f-5c36-4918-8745-c6acd9316f40R01